AF655220

World of Wonder

LIVING WORLD

Author: Gerard Cheshire has written many books on natural history, and over the past twelve years has cultivated an excellent reputation as an author and editor. He now lives in Bath, England, with his wife and three sons.

Artists: Janet Baker (JB Illustrations), Mark Bergin, John Francis, Nick Hewetson, Pam Hewetson, Li Sidong, Emily Mayer, Terry Riley, Carolyn Scrace

Editor: Stephen Haynes

Editorial assistants: Rob Walker, Tanya Kant

ISBN-13: 978-93-5275-490-8

This edition: June 2018

Reprinted by Scholastic India Pvt. Ltd.

Printed at Acme Tradex India Pvt. Ltd.

World of Wonder

Living World

by

Gerard Cheshire

SCHOLASTIC

NEW YORK • TORONTO • LONDON • AUCKLAND • SYDNEY
NEW DELHI • HONG KONG

Contents

Why Is the Living World Special? 5

What's the Biggest Creature on Earth? 6

What Are the Fastest Animals on Earth? 8

What's the Tallest Creature Ever? 10

What's the Deadliest Creature on Earth? 12

What's the Oldest Living Thing? 14

What's the World's Tallest Tree? 16

What's the Largest Insect? 18

What's the Biggest Bird? 20

What's the Most Intelligent Animal? 22

Who Has the Scariest Teeth? 24

What's the Most Endangered Species? 26

Who Makes the Longest Land Migration? 28

Useful Words 30

Answers 31

Index 32

Why Is the Living World Special?

The world around us is filled with living things. So far there are 1.7 million **species** known to science, and they come in all shapes, sizes, colors, and patterns. Without the different animals and plants that make up the living world, we humans could not survive.

Rain forests have more species than any other kind of **habitat**. In fact, new species are being discovered every year.

What's the Biggest Creature on Earth?

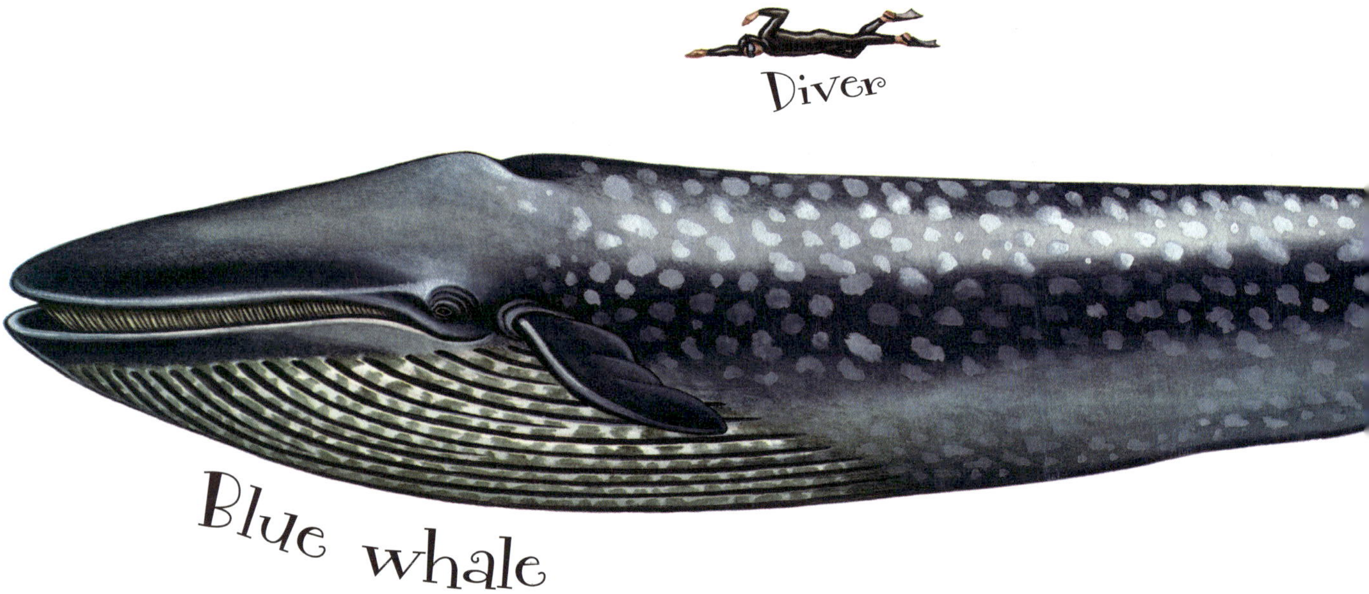

The blue whale is the biggest animal on earth. Even the biggest dinosaurs didn't grow as large as the blue whale. The blue whale lives in the ocean, and the water helps to carry its huge weight. The blue whale can grow up to 110 feet (33 m) long and weigh 200 tons (180 metric tons).

Reticulated python

The reticulated python is one of the world's longest snakes, and can grow up to 26 feet (8 m) long.

True or False?

Most bacteria are so small that you can't see them without a microscope.

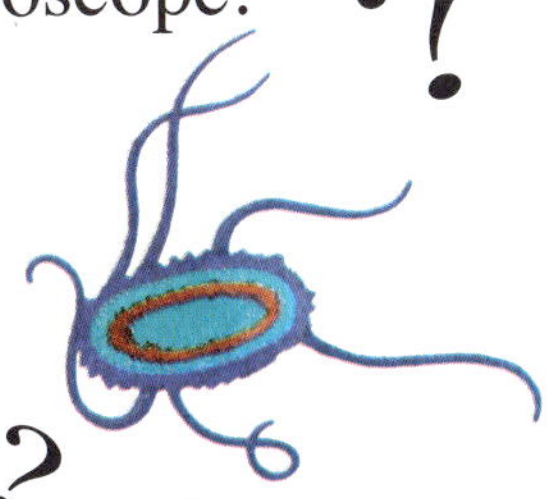

Answers on page 31

African elephant

The largest land animal is the African elephant. It is big enough to tear down trees to eat the leaves and bark. It has a large stomach, too, so it can digest large amounts of vegetation. Its size helps to scare off **predators** such as lions and hyenas.

What Are the Fastest Animals on Earth?

The fastest land animal is the cheetah. This big cat hunts fast-moving animals like antelope. A cheetah's top speed is about 70 miles (113 km) per hour, but it can run quickly only for a minute or so. After that, it has to slow down and rest.

What's the fastest fish?

The sailfish is the world's fastest fish. It can swim up to 65 miles (105 km) per hour when hunting. When a sailfish swims very fast, it folds down the sail-like fin on its back so that it can slip through the water more quickly.

A need for speed!

Predators are animals that eat other animals. Some predators use their great speed to chase their **prey**. Other predators ambush their prey—they creep up on them and strike by surprise.

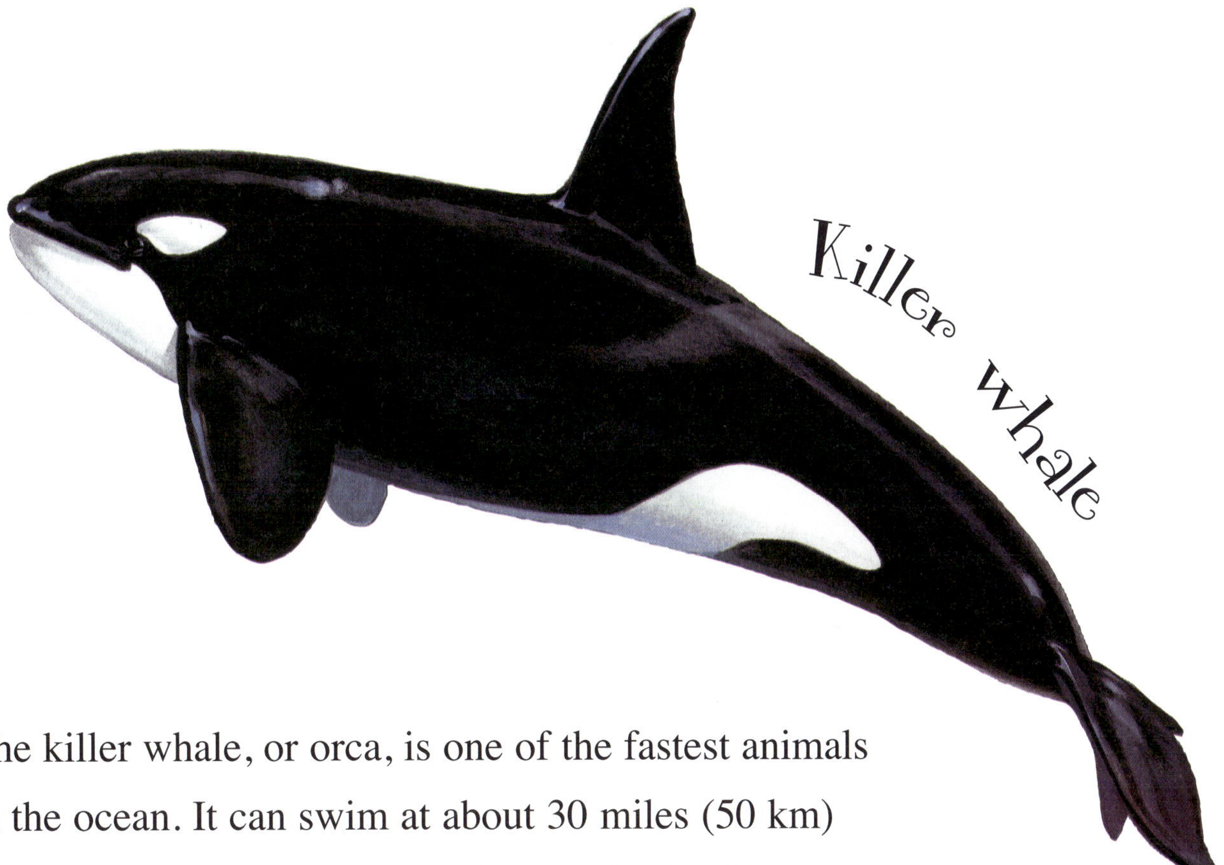

The killer whale, or orca, is one of the fastest animals in the ocean. It can swim at about 30 miles (50 km) per hour. Killer whales swim thousands of miles looking for food such as seals and fish. They can be found in all of the world's oceans.

One of the tallest animals that ever lived was a dinosaur called Brachiosaurus. It stood about 39 feet (12 m) high and was 80 feet (25 m) long. It weighed more than 33 tons (30 metric tons).

Brachiosaurus lived around 150 million years ago. Its great height allowed it to reach leaves on tall trees.

A dinosaur called Sauroposeidon was probably even taller. So far scientists have found only a few of its neck bones, but they can figure out from these how tall it is likely to have been.

True or False?

Seismosaurus is the longest dinosaur so far discovered.

Answers on page 31

What's the tallest living animal?

The tallest land animal alive today is the giraffe. Giraffes are about three times the height of humans. They can be up to 18 feet (5.5 m) high. Their height enables them to eat the leaves that elephants and antelopes cannot reach.

How does a human measure up?

Compared with giraffes and large dinosaurs, humans are short. But we can use tools such as ladders or cranes to reach high things.

What's the Deadliest Creature on Earth?

Animals may be dangerous in different ways. Some spread poison when they sting and bite. Others kill by spreading diseases. The most dangerous of all is the mosquito, which kills more than a million people every year. This is because the bites of some mosquitoes can give people a deadly disease called malaria.

Are frogs poisonous?

Some frogs are poisonous to people and other animals. Many poisonous frogs have bright colors that warn other animals not to eat them. In the rain forest of South America live brightly colored frogs known as poison arrow frogs. Hunters collect the poison from the frogs' skin and use it on the tips of their arrows.

Mosquitoes

A mosquito has a needle-like mouth called a **proboscis**, which it uses to pierce the skin and drink the blood of people or animals. Humans are easy to bite because we don't have thick fur or scales to protect us.

Cobra

How many people die of snakebites?

Thousands of people around the world die from snakebites every year. In **tropical** countries, snakes often slither into people's homes. They will bite anyone who accidentally steps on them or bothers them.

True or False?

The Brazilian wandering spider has the most deadly **venom** in the world.

Answers on page 31

What's the Oldest Living Thing?

The bristlecone pine tree, found in the southern United States, is one of the world's oldest living **organisms**. Some bristlecone pines are almost 5,000 years old and are still growing.

The trunk of a tree grows a new layer, or ring, every year of its life. Scientists can tell the age of a tree by counting the rings.

Usually, the animals and plants that live longest are the ones that grow most slowly.

Bristlecone pine tree

True or False?

The oldest sea creature is 300 years old.

Answers on page 31

What's the oldest land animal?

The longest-living land animals are the giant tortoises. They have been known to live for up to 200 years. A Galápagos tortoise named Harriet, who lived at the Australian Zoo, died in 2006 at the age of about 175.

Giant tortoises

Legend has it that scientist Charles Darwin found Harriet as a young tortoise in 1835.

What's the World's Tallest Tree?

The tallest tree is a coast redwood in California, which is 379 feet (115.5 m) tall—that's around 65 times as tall as an adult human. Its exact location is kept secret to protect it from damage by tourists. In a forest, the tallest trees get the most sunlight.

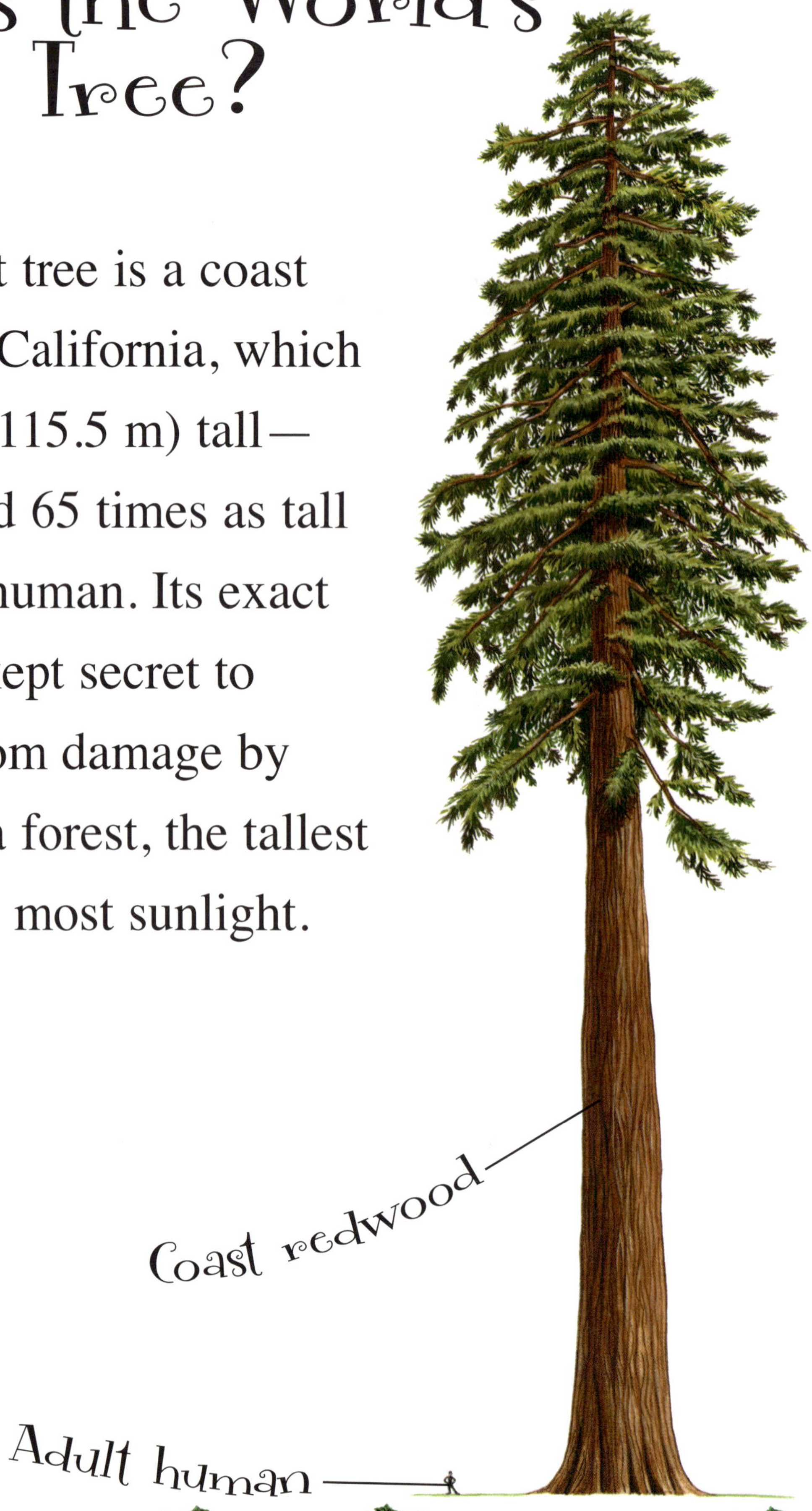

True or False?

The second-tallest type of tree, the coast Douglas fir, reaches 326 feet (99.4 m)—taller than the Statue of Liberty.

Answers on page 31

What's the biggest flower?

The Titan arum is a lily with the largest flower in the world. The flower can be 9 feet (2.75 m) tall and 4 feet (1.2 m) wide.

What's the smelliest plant?

The Titan arum stinks like rotting flesh. The smell attracts flies. The flies then **pollinate** the flowers. The female flowers later become fruit. Birds eat the fruit and drop the seeds, and new plants grow.

What's the Largest Insect?

One of the largest beetles is the Hercules beetle, which can be 6.75 inches (17 cm) long. Male Hercules beetles have huge horns. They use these to fight other males for a mate. They live in hot, humid places, such as the rain forests of South and Central America.

What's the longest insect?

The longest insect ever measured was a giant stick insect. It was an amazing 22 inches (55 cm) long, including its outstretched legs. Many giant stick insects grow to more than 12 inches (30 cm) long.

There are many different species of stick insect. Most live in hot places such as the jungles of Southeast Asia. Their stick-like shape gives them very good **camouflage**.

Stick insect hiding in leaves

Hercules beetle

Shown actual size

What was the largest insect ever?

True or False?

The Goliath bird-eating spider from South America is the size of a dinner plate.

Answers on page 31

The largest insect that ever lived was a giant dragonfly called a Meganeurid, which had a wingspan of 29.5 inches (75 cm). It lived about 300 million years ago. These days insects do not grow quite as big, because there is less oxygen in the air. Insects don't have lungs, so they can't get oxygen from the air as easily as other animals can.

What's the Biggest Bird?

The African ostrich is the world's tallest and heaviest bird. It can be 9 feet (2.7 m) tall and weigh up to 285 pounds (130 kg). The giant moa of New Zealand and the elephant birds of Madagascar were much bigger, but these birds are now **extinct**.

What bird has the longest wingspan?

The wandering albatross, from the islands of the Antarctic ocean, has the largest wingspan—more than 10 feet (3 m) from tip to tip. Albatrosses can glide great distances over the oceans without flapping their long, narrow wings. This helps them to save valuable energy.

What bird has the longest bill?

The Australian pelican has the longest bill of any bird. The longest ever measured was 19 inches (49 cm) long. The bird grows up to 6 feet (1.8 m) long, so the bill is almost a third of the bird's total length.

What's the Most Intelligent Animal?

Of course, humans believe that they are the most intelligent species. The next most intelligent are the great apes—gorillas, orangutans, chimpanzees, and bonobos. But many animals can do certain things as well as humans can.

Squirrels sometimes trick other animals by pretending to hide food. Some dolphins have learned to use sponges to protect their noses from sharp corals. Some pigs are said to be good at video games!

Which animal has the largest brain?

Whales and elephants have bigger brains than ours. A human brain weighs about 3.3 pounds (1.5 kg), while that of an African elephant weighs about 16.5 pounds (7.5 kg). But if you compare the size of an animal's brain to the size of its body, then humans have the largest brains. Scientists say that this makes us the smartest species.

African elephant

Sperm whale

True or False?

Some birds use sticks to get at grubs hiding in branches.

Answers on page 31

Human being

Humans are the only species capable of communicating by using spoken and written language. Some apes have been taught by humans to use simple sign language.

Who Has the Scariest Teeth?

Sperm whales have long, narrow mouths filled with lots of pointed teeth for catching squid and fish. The sperm whale is one of the largest **carnivores** (meat-eaters) in the ocean, and its mouth is around 16 feet (5 m) long. Its prey may include the giant squid, which can be over 40 feet (12 m) long.

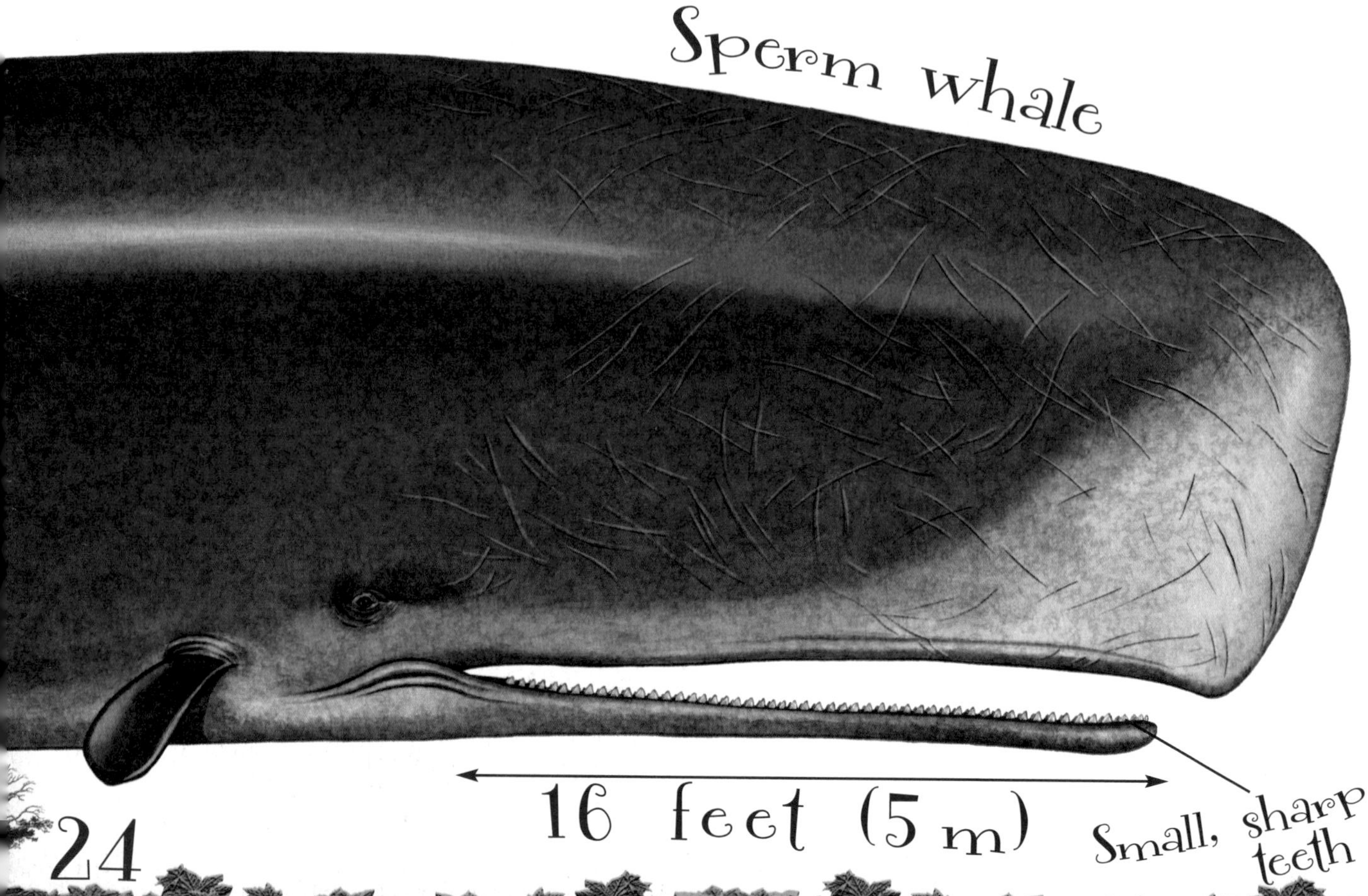

Tusks or teeth?

The hippopotamus has a huge mouth, complete with a set of very scary tusks. These tusks are actually long **canine teeth**. Male hippos have the longest tusks; they use them to fight other males. Although hippos are **herbivores** (plant-eaters), they are very aggressive and have been known to attack and kill people when they feel threatened.

True or False?

The giant squid has the largest eyes in the world.

Answers on page 31

What's the Most Endangered Species?

The black rhinoceros is one of the world's most **endangered** species. It is hunted for its horns, which some people believe can be used to make medicine. Now there are only around 3,000 black rhinos left in the wild, and nearly all of these live in protected areas.

The giant panda is endangered because it can live only in a habitat called a bamboo forest. Because much of the bamboo forest has been destroyed, giant pandas now live only in a few mountain areas in China. Another problem is that pandas have very few cubs.

Giant panda

Tiger

Many species become extinct every year without many people noticing. These are often small animals or plants that are not as well known as bigger animals like tigers and pandas.

Tigers are endangered because people kill them or destroy parts of their habitat. Some tigers are hunted. Others are killed because they are dangerous to people and cattle. Many forests where tigers once lived have been cut down. There may now be more tigers in zoos and reserves than there are in the wild.

True or False?

The Scots pine is an endangered tree species.

Answers on page 31

Who Makes the Longest Land Migration?

Migration is the movement of animals to a different place for part of the year. The longest migration on land is made by the caribou of North America. Each spring, thousands of caribou travel as far as 3,100 miles (5,000 km) to the Arctic to look for food and to rear their young.

In winter, the caribou go south again.

In Europe, caribou are called "reindeer."

Spur-winged goose

Every year, the spur-winged goose completes a marathon migration from Europe or Asia to Africa and back again. The geese migrate when the weather turns cold and food becomes scarce.

True or False?

The humpback whale travels 2,500 miles (4,000 km) in one trip.

Useful words

Camouflage Special markings, shapes, or coloring on an animal that help the animal blend in with its surroundings.

Canine teeth The pointed teeth that are one each side of the front teeth in humans and many other animals.

Carnivore An animal that eats mostly meat.

Endangered At risk of dying out.

Extinct No longer alive anywhere in the world.

Habitat The place where a particular type of plant or animal lives naturally.

Herbivore An animal that eats mostly plants.

Migration The movement of animals to a different part of the world for part of the year.

Organism A living thing.

Pollinate To help plants reproduce by carrying pollen from one plant to another.

Predator An animal that hunts and kills other animals for food.

Prey An animal killed and eaten by another animal.

Proboscis The needle-like mouth of an insect or other animal. Mosquitoes use it to puncture the skin.

Rain forest A dense forest with high rainfall.

Species A group of living things that look alike, behave in the same way, and produce young that do the same.

Tropical Having to do with the tropics—the hot, rainy area between the Tropic of Cancer and the Tropic of Capricorn.

Venom A poison produced by an animal.

Answers

Page 7 TRUE! Most types of bacteria are far too small to see with the naked eye. Thousands of them could fit on a pinhead.

Page 11 TRUE! Scientists think that the Seismosaurus reached 150 feet (45 m) in length.

Page 13 TRUE! The bite of the Brazilian wandering spider causes swelling, fevers, and breathing problems. It can sometimes lead to death in people. The strong venom prevents the spider's prey from running away.

Page 15 FALSE! The oldest sea creatures ever discovered were deep-sea corals that were up to 4,000 years old.

Page 17 TRUE! The Statue of Liberty is only 305 feet (93 m) tall.

Page 19 TRUE! The bird-eating spider is a kind of tarantula. It has a 12-inch (30-cm) leg span.

Page 23 TRUE! Galápagos finches poke with sticks to find grubs hiding in tree bark.

Page 25 TRUE! The giant squid's eyes can be up to 16 inches (40 cm) in diameter.

Page 27 FALSE! Scots pine is not endangered, but many other trees are. Big-leaf mahogany, for example, is cut down for its valuable timber and new trees are not always planted to replace the old ones.

Page 29 FALSE! The humpback migrates almost 3,100 miles (5,000 km).

Giant tortoises

Index

(Illustrations are shown in **bold type**.)

African elephant **7, 23**
ape **22**
Australian pelican **21**

bacteria **7**
black rhinoceros **26**
blue whale **6**
bonobo 22
Brachiosaurus **10**
Brazilian wandering spider **13**
Bristlecone pine tree **14**

camouflage 18
caribou **28–29**
cheetah **8–9**
chimpanzee **22**
clam **15**
coast Douglas fir **17**
coast redwood **16**
cobra **13**

Darwin, Charles 15
dinosaur 6, 10
dolphin **22**
dragonfly 19

elephant *see* African elephant

Galápagos finch **23**, 31
giant panda **27**
giant squid **24–25**
giant tortoise **15**
giraffe **11**
Goliath bird-eating spider **19**
gorilla 22

Harriet (giant tortoise) 15
Hercules beetle 18–**19**
hippopotamus **25**
human being **11**, **16**, 22–23
humpback whale **29**

killer whale **9**

Meganeurid 19
migration 28–29
moa 20
mosquito **12**–13

North America 28

orangutan 22
ostrich **20**

poison arrow frog 13

rain forest **5,** 13, 18
reindeer **28–29**
reticulated python **7**

sailfish **8**
Sauroposeidon 10

Scots pine 27
Seismosaurus **11**
South America 13, 18–19
sperm whale **23, 24**
spur-winged goose **29**
squirrel **22**
Statue of Liberty **17**
stick insect **18**

tiger **27**
Titan Arum **17**

wandering albatross **21**

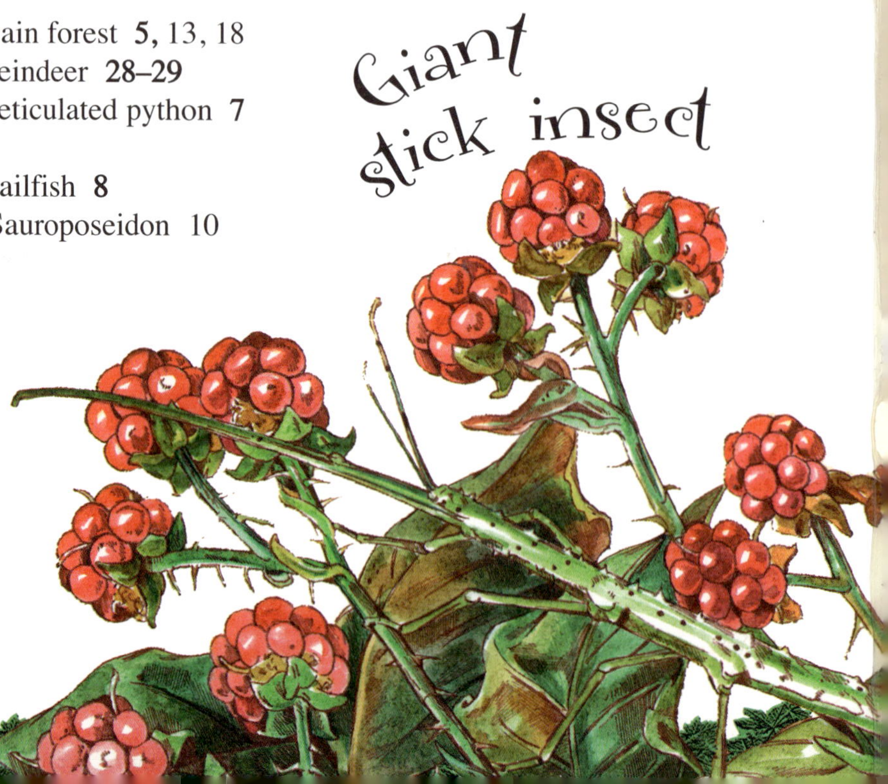